c

D1437310

THE BATMAN STRIKES!

Raintree is an imprint of Capstone Global Library
Limited, a company incorporated in England and
Wales having its registered office at 7 Pilgrim Street,
London, EC4V 6LB - Registered company number:
6695582

First published by Raintree in 2014
The moral rights of the proprietor have been
asserted.

Originally published by DC Comics in the US in single
magazine form as The Batman Strikes! #1.
Copyright © 2014 DC Comics. All Rights Reserved.

Ashley C. Andersen Zantop *Publisher*
Michael Dahl *Editorial Director*
Sean Tulien *Editor*
Heather Kindseth *Creative Director*
Bob Lentz *Designer*
Kathy McColley *Production Specialist*

DC COMICS

Joan Hilty & Harvey Richards *Original U.S. Editors*
Jeff Matsuda & Dave McCaig *Cover Artists*

ISBN 978 1 406 27961 0

Printed in China by Nordica
1013/CA21301918
17 16 15 14 13
10 9 8 7 6 5 4 3 2 1

British Library Cataloguing in Publication Data
A full catalogue record for this book is
available from the British Library.

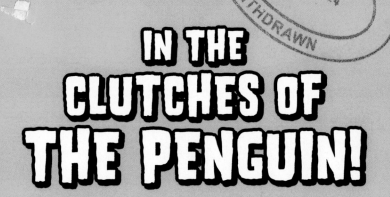

IN THE CLUTCHES OF THE PENGUIN!

BILL MATHENY ....WRITER
CHRISTOPHER JONES ....PENCILLER
TERRY BEATTY...INKER
HEROIC AGE..COLOURIST
PAT BROSSEAU ....LETTERER

BATMAN CREATED BY BOB KANE

PENGUIN RISING

BILL MATHENY-WRITER
CHRISTOPHER JONES-PENCILLER
TERRY BEATTY-INKER
PAT BROSSEAU-LETTERER
HEROIC AGE-COLORIST
HARVEY RICHARDS-ASST EDITOR
JOAN HILTY-EDITOR
BATMAN CREATED BY BOB KANE

WHAT IN...

WATCH THE *LANGUAGE*, MY DEAR FELLOW! DON'T MAKE ME TAKE WHAT'S LEFT OF YOU UP TO THE OFFICE AND FILE A *COMPLAINT*!

SEIZE HIM, MY *KABUKI TWINS*!

NOW, I NEED YOUR HELP TO PREPARE MY...WELL, CALL IT A *PERSONAL THANK-YOU* TO THAT MILLIONAIRE SNOT *BRUCE WAYNE*!

WHERE *IS* HE, ANYWAY?

SIR, THIS *ISN'T* A MUSIC STORE! THOSE *CLASSIC GUITARS* ARE WORTH A FORTUNE, AND THEY'RE THE PROPERTY OF *BRUCE...*

6

AWK!

LADIES, WE HAVE A VISITOR-- THE *BAT* WHO WISHES HE WERE A *BIRD!*

GIVE ME THE UMBRELLA AND YOU CAN KEEP THE ARM, *PENGUIN!*

I BELIEVE I'D RATHER *KEEP* THE ARM AND *LOSE* THE *BAT!*

BLEW! BLEW!

PTING PTING PTING

OH, PLEASE.

KABUKI IS SO *19TH* CENTURY.

WHUD

CHOK

THESE DETECTIVE TYPES ARE ALL THE SAME. HAVE *BACKHAND*, WILL *CRUMBLE!*

THE WAYNE FAMILY *LAUGHED* AT THE COBBLEPOTS! TRIED TO *DESTROY* US!

BUT THEY COULDN'T--AND *PAYBACK'S A REAL BEAK!*

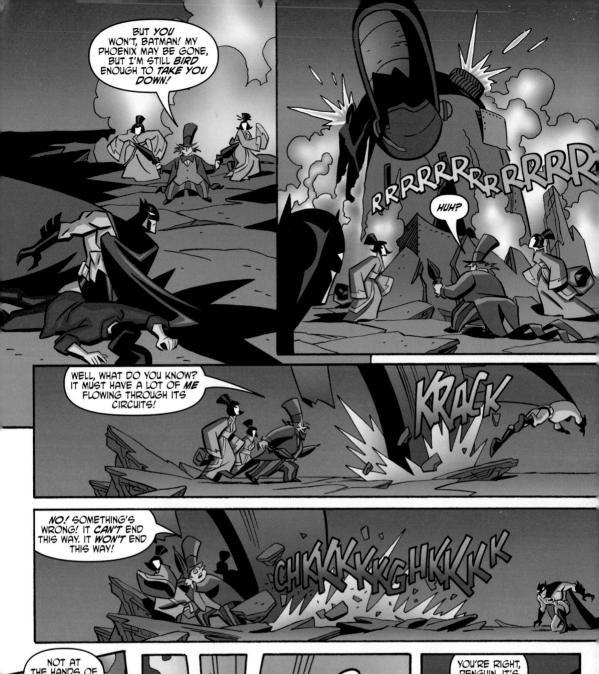

CREATORS

BILL MATHENY WRITER
Along with comics such as THE BATMAN STRIKES, Bill Matheny has written for
TV series including KRYPTO THE SUPERDOG, WHERE'S WALDO, A PUP NAMED
SCOOBY-DOO, and many others.

CHRISTOPHER JONES PENCILLER
Christopher Jones is an artist who has worked for DC Comics, Image, Malibu,
Caliber, and Sundragon Comics.

TERRY BEATTY INKER
Terry Beatty has inked THE BATMAN STRIKES! and BATMAN: THE BRAVE AND THE
BOLD as well as several other DC Comics graphic novels.

GLOSSARY

acknowledging greeting someone

analysis process of studying something very closely

artefact object from the past that was made or changed by human beings

curator person in charge of a museum or art gallery

dedicated gave a lot of energy and time to something or someone

kabuki type of Japanese drama traditionally performed by men in elaborate costumes

oaf fool

obnoxious very unpleasant, annoying, or offensive

tacky cheap or corny

trajectory arc that objects travel

vigilante someone who takes the law into their own hands

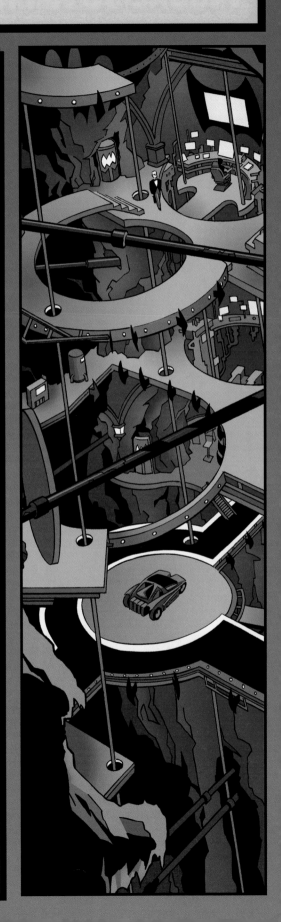

VISUAL QUESTIONS & PROMPTS

1. Batman uses many tools to fight crime. Here he uses a batarang attached to a rope to grab hold of the Penguin. Design a new tool for Batman. What does it do? How does it work?

2. Based on these two panels, what do you think the bat-wave technology does? Explain your answer using examples from the book.

AWK!

LADIES, WE HAVE A VISITOR-- THE *BAT* WHO WISHES HE WERE A *BIRD!*

GIVE ME THE UMBRELLA AND YOU CAN KEEP THE ARM, *PENGUIN!*

1

CLEVER B... HE'S USING *BAT-WAVE TECHNOLOGY* TO TRY TO CAUSE A ONE-MILE...

2

"...BLACKOUT!"

BEEP
BEEP
BEEP

3. Batman's symbol represents his super hero identity. Create your own super hero symbol. Is it based on an animal or something else? What would you choose for your super hero name?

3

4. The artists of this book added lines to this panel. Why did they do that? How does it make the panel feel?

4

READ THEM ALL!